With Compliments

BERGEN

THE GATEWAY TO
THE FJORDS OF NORWAY

CONTENTS

BERGEN

MOUNTAINS AND FJORDS

Bergen is known as "The City Between Seven Mountains". Now, however, it has also become the proud bearer of the name "The City Between Seven Fjords" — a change which came about in 1972 when the administrative region of Bergen was merged with four surrounding districts to become the district of Bergen in the administrative region of Hordaland.

"It's crowded here in among the mountains" a Bergen poet once wrote — and it did get crowded! The city's population figures increased steadily over the centuries, partly due to an influx of outsiders, not least the Hansas. The city grew from the eastern side of Vågen round to the west and southwards down the valley. There, after the last war, new

parts of the city were built — it was, after all, getting rather cramped in the old city. 1955 saw Bergen breaking southwestwards through the mountains into the area of Fyllingsdalen. It was touch and go as to whether it would remain Norway's second largest city, but then came 1972 with its administrative reorganisation and the figures doubled!

The Ulriken cable-car.

It will come as a surprise to many to hear that a good 40% of Bergen's 465 square kilometres is wooded, with the mountains making up 21%. But it is the mountains and fjords which have shaped Bergen, and which are the subject of innumerable songs. The sea was a source of trade and a link with the rest of the world – a world beyond, which the people of

Bergen were more in touch with than other parts of Norway. Geographically, the city turned its back on the rest of the country – only with the opening of the Bergen railway in 1909 did it really become part of Norway.

The mountains which until then had closed off the city became public areas – in the old days as grazing land, more recently as a source of

recreation. The locals don't have far to go to get out into the country, and even less so these days. 1918 saw the opening of Fløibanen, the funicular railway running up to the top of Mount Fløyen – just as much a link to the suburbs for those living on the mountainside as a means of transport for walkers heading for the city's most popular mountain, also one of

Bergen's biggest tourist attractions.
Then came Ulriksbanen in 1961, a
cable car to the city's highest and
"sacred" mountain and also something of a tourist attraction in its
own right. The views from the top
are magnificent and once up in the
mountains, walkers have a wonderful
variety of walks and paths to choose
from.

ALIVE WITH THE PAST

Bergen is immediately identifiable by its profile - the pointed gables of Bryggen. Included on UNESCO's World Heritage List, Bryggen was once the heart (not to mention the stomach) of the city and, together with Vågsbunnen, forms the oldest part of Bergen. Nevertheless, it's very much alive and kicking!

During the Middle Ages Bryggen stretched from where the Korskirken church now stands down as far as Bergenhus. Later the area was short- ened and widened as Vågen was filled in and new quays were built. Bryggen's houses were designed to ensure that most of them could have their own stretch of shore. That's how things stood when the hanseatic merchants arrived, and that's how they still stand, though these days Bryggen's wooden houses date back no further than 1702 when a fire razed most of Bergen to the ground. However, the houses were rebuilt as exact replicas, and those which were ravaged by two fires in the 1950s were also rebuilt as careful copies. The only thing to have changed is the most southern area where, at the

Bryggen with Fløyen in the background.

beginning of the century, the people of Bergen managed to agree on a new district plan, tore down the wooden houses and replaced them with tall brick houses. But with the pointed gables facing the sea, retaining Bergen's profile.

Trading is still a way of life on Bryggen, though dried fish is decidedly less popular! These days the colourful line of buildings houses an abundance of small shops, restaurants, craftsmen, galleries and even a small museum. Anyone interested in finding out how Bergen's forefathers lived should visit the Hanseatic Museum at the southern end and the Schøtstuene assembly rooms behind Bryggen. Here is a chance to see how merchants and their servants lived day to day, and delve into their social comings and goings.

Bryggen has seen many an excavation project and some of the finds are on show in the Bryggen Museum to the north of the wooden houses, a centre for medieval archaeology. This area is also home to the Mariakirken church which, dating back to the twelfth century, is Bergen's

oldest preserved building. In the Middle Ages Bergen had a wealth of churches, but only three have survived: the Domkirken (Cathedral), the Korskirken and the Mariakirken, which is the best preserved, the other two being considerably altered over the centuries. The hanseatic merchants took over the Mariakirken for their own use and furnished it richly – a late Gothic wooden altar from the end of the fifteenth century and a magnificent Baroque pulpit donated to the church in 1676.

A little further north lies Holmen, Norway's power centre in the twelfth and thirteenth centuries, today known as Bergenhus. Even after the king had headed east to Oslo, Holmen remained the ecclesiastical, secular and military centre of western Norway. The large Kristkirken and other smaller churches in the area are long gone, but the stone hall which Håkon Håkonsson built to celebrate his son Magnus' wedding and coronation in 1261, possibly with the help of English craftsmen, stands to this very

day. In the Middle Ages the hall saw a number of coronations, royal weddings and important political meetings, but was then ravaged over time and ultimately used as a warehouse. 700 years after the first celebrations it was the subject of a royal visit once more – by which time it had been restored after the considerable damage sustained in an explosion in 1944, the worst catastrophe to strike Bergen during the war. These days the Håkonshall is the finest hall in Bergen and is widely used for concerts.

The other striking stone building in Bergenhus is the Rosenkrantz Tower, named after Erik Rosenkrantz who was the king's representative in Bergen in the middle of the sixteenth century. He converted Magnus Lagabøte's thirteenth century fortress tower to a residence with a Renaissance facade facing the city. The canons at the top of the tower also faced Bergen, pointing towards the hanseatic traders who gradually lost their power, thanks to the king's dynamic representatives.

Girl dressed in national costume
from the Bergen region.

Bryggen i Bergen offers a
wide selection of shops.

The narrow alleys of Bryggen.

Schøtstuene, the 16th/17th-century Hanseatic Assembly Rooms on Bryggen.

HANSEATIC CITY

Bergen is sometimes referred to as a hanseatic city. While not strictly true, this sounds undeniably grander than "office city" which is what it was for the Hanseatic League, the German association of merchants which dominated north European trade during the Middle Ages, and which also had contacts in the Mediterranean.

Bergen traded in a commodity which was increasingly in demand in thirteenth century Europe – dried fish from northern Norway. However, the Hansas gradually came to dominate, taking over more and more of the foreign trade in a complex political game where the kings initially tried to stem the power of the hanseatic merchants. To no avail – the

merchants ended up with both privileges and a monopoly on the trade of dried fish out of the city. From the middle of the fourteenth century the League set up an office in Bergen – one of the four main offices along with London, Novgorod and Bruges.

The hanseatic merchants initially rented houses on the Bryggen wharf, and then went on to buy them. This

Room in the Hanseatic Museum.

explains why Bryggen is sometimes referred to as hanseatic, though the houses were already there when the Germans arrived. Bryggen does not, in other words, have hanseatic origins. The merchants were based there for around 400 years, though their power and influence waned from the mid-1500s onwards. A selfgoverning, purely male society, they were not supposed to mingle with the locals – nevertehless there was lots of wine, women and song in the stretch behind Bryggen. When the Hanseatic League's power came to an end, the merchants had the option of returning to their own country or settling in Norway – many chose the latter, the result being some of Bergen's "good old" families and names.

Zakariasbryggen, a hive of activity.

The Dragon Boat Festival

Children playing at Ole Bulls plass.

"Den Blå Steinen" (The Blue Stone) at Ole Bulls Plass is a meeting place for people in Bergen.

Christian VII's monogram on the Old Town Hall recalls the king who was expected to visit but never came.

Håkonshallen, King Håkon Håkonsson's magnificent banqueting hall.

From Bergenhus Castle.

The Rosenkrantz Tower.

Interior of the Rosenkrantz Tower.

The Cathedral.

*Mariakirken, dating back to the 12th century, is Bergen's oldest building.
The tabernacle in Mariakirken (St Mary's Church) is one of Bergen's greatest ecclesiastical treasures.*

Fantoft stave church.

The stave church is a highly advanced type of churches known from the Christian period of the Middle Ages in Norway and is Norway's most significant contribution to European architechture.

Fantoft stave church was moved from the small community Fortun in Sogn to Consul Gade's farm in Fantoft in 1883.

After being totally destroyed by a fire in June 1992, Fantoft stave church was rebuilt from the drawings of architect Kjell Irgens. He was also given the assignment of designing a copy of a stave church (Holt Ålens stave church) as a gift from Norway to Iceland in the occasion of the 1000th anniversary.

In 1837 Norwegian artist J.C.

Dahl published the work *Denkmale einer sehr ausgebildeten Holzbaukunst,* which deals with the distinctive features of the stave churches and their architectural significance.

Bergen's famous fish market is an experience in itself.

Bergen Aquarium.

FISH AND FORTIFICATION

With the exception of the Fantoft stave church, Edvard Grieg's home Troldhaugen and Ole Bull's island villa on Lysøen, everything in Bergen is within easy striking distance of the centre.

Many visitors begin at the city's fish market at Fisketorget where they are tempted by salmon, prawns, crabs and other delicacies from the

deep. From here it is but a hop, skip and a jump to the Fløibanen funicular railway, Bryggen, Bergenhus and the Mariakirken. And to the yellow bus which goes out to the delightful Gamle Bergen (Old Bergen) open air museum, just a ten minute drive away.

But other parts of the city centre are also worth investigating – a little

to the south lies Det Gamle Rådhus, the old city hall where the people's representatives have met since the middle of the 1500s. On the other side of the high-rise modern block which has been Bergen's City Hall since 1974 stands a large, white-washed building: Manufakturhuset – Bergen's largest secular brick house in the Baroque style. Having started

out as a workhouse, it now serves as council offices. Further south, in the small area of Marken, is the St. Jørgen Hospital. Named in 1409, it was, until recent times, a hospital for lepers and had its own church. As such, it is appropriate that it currently houses, among other things, the world's only leprosy museum.

The Nordnes peninsula separates Vågen from the Pudde Fjord, and has links with both fish and fortresses. At the very end of the peninsula is the Aquarium, one of Bergen's greatest attractions. Opened in 1960, it was financed by local fund-raising – nothing new to Bergen with its tradition of generous patrons and city folk who collect

money for everything from the Maritime Museum and the University Library to the Aquarium and the Grieghallen.

Nordnes is also home to Fredriksberg, a small fortress dating back to the 1660s, built after the 1665 battle between the English and the Dutch in Vågen, and also one of Bergen's former execution sites.

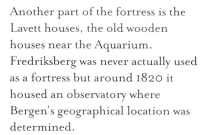

Another part of the fortress is the Lavett houses, the old wooden houses near the Aquarium. Fredriksberg was never actually used as a fortress but around 1820 it housed an observatory where Bergen's geographical location was determined.

The weather is not always fine in Bergen!

Grieghallen (concert hall).

CITY OF CULTURE

In a city where the title of "merchant" really meant something, it's hardly surprising that many an accusation has been levelled at the locals over the centuries for wrapping themselves up in their trading and shipping, dried fish and accounts.

Although there's no smoke without fire, the people of Bergen did actually see beyond their trading.

Ever since the twelfth and thirteenth centuries when it was the capital of Norway, Bergen has attracted foreigners with the result that its merchants were not unaware of what was going on in Europe. They picked up on trends and ideas and were eventually rich enough to breathe life into these ideas. Sober in their day-to-day business,

they really went to town elsewhere: building pavilions, designing gardens along foreign lines, enjoying music, reading, and indulging in the theatre.

1765 saw the foundation of "Musikselskabet Harmonien", the origins of today's Bergen Philharmonic Orchestra, one of the oldest symphony orchestras in the world.

King Harald and Queen Sonja arriving at the Bergen International Festival.

Gamlehaugen, Bergen's royal residence.

In 1850 violin virtuoso and local lad Ole Bull founded Norway's first national theatre where both Henrik Ibsen and Bjørnstjerne Bjørnson cut their dramatic teeth as play-wrights and instructors. Scandi-navia's first major comedy play-wright, Ludvig Holberg, spent most of his life in Copenhagen, but was originally from Bergen and also wrote a famous book describing the city in his day. Norway's first impor-tant landscape painter, J. C. Dahl, came from Bergen - and the fact that Edvard Grieg was also a local was the reasoning behind the Bergen International Festival. Since the very first festival in 1953, early summer in Bergen has been transformed into what King Olav in his time termed "a cultural Mecca" in Norway. "In other words, the city has the royal seal as a city of culture — and was also given the seal as a Euro-pean City of Culture in the year 2000.

Ole Bull's home on the island of Lysøen, in the neighbouring district of Os.

In 1885 Grieg purchased Troldhaugen, a lovely Swiss-style villa on the shores of Nordåsvannet. From then until his death, Grieg spent every summer at Troldhaugen.

Interior view of Troldhaugen.

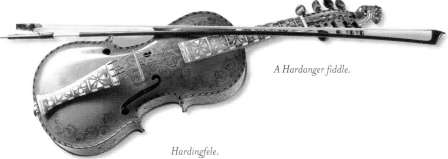

A Hardanger fiddle.

Hardingfele.

Edvard Grieg's music is a bridge between Norway and Europe. His works represent a blend of the European classical tradition and Norwegian folk music which was unique in its day. Edvard Grieg was born in Bergen in 1843 and died in 1907.

"Nina and Edvard Grieg at the piano". Painting by P.S. Krøyer, 1898.

Sheet of music,
"The Death of Åse".

"Birch in Storm", J.C. Dahl, 1849.

ART MUSEUMS

Like every city, Bergen has its fair share of museums and art collections. Two are, however, unique: The Leprosy Museum and the Buekorps Museum. The latter is housed in Muren on Nordnes – a stone building dating from the sixteenth century resembling a town gate. The building itself was originally used for celebrations on the

first floor and by farmers for trading on the ground floor. The museum, which is open at weekends, tells the story of the city's buekorps, a type of boys' brigade, which was set up in the middle of the last century. These days the buekorps is a phenomenon confined to Bergen, but has had offshoots in many Norwegian cities.

Also unique – and impressive –

is the sizeable China collection at the Vestlandske Kunstindustrimuseum. The collection of art, fabrics and other objects was donated by Bergen General J. W. N. Munthe who lived in China from 1887 and who, among other things, helped modernise the Chinese army.

Another gift to Bergen was Rasmus Meyer's collection of paint-

Bergen Art Museum has taken over the old power station (Bergen Lysverker), and the art from Bergen Art Gallery (Bergen Billedgalleri) has gotten its own arena. The first exhibition "Past masters — Norwegian Classics" opened in May 2000, showing a.o. paintings by J. C. Dahl and Edward Munch.

The boys' archery corps are a Bergen tradition.

ings, furniture and interiors which was housed in its own building on Lille Lungegårdsvann, the small lake in the centre of Bergen, in 1924. At the heart of the collection lie Norwegian paintings spanning from J. C. Dahl to Edvard Munch, who is represented through many of his main works. The collections also include rococo interiors with their ceiling and wall paintings. Bergen has also received donations from people living outside the city, Rolf Stenersen being one such patron — his collection has been placed in Bergen Billedgalleri and, of course, includes paintings by the city's greatest painter J. C. Dahl, for example the well-known "Birch in a storm".

THE WOODEN CITY

While Bergen's archives boast an impressive collection of city plans, it is fire that has had more of an impact than any planners ever did. Apart from various public buildings made of stone, Bergen grew up over the centuries as a city of wooden buildings only to be devoured by fire at regular intervals. The worst was, perhaps, the great fire of 1702 which took most of the city with it. The most expensive was the fire of 1916 – known as the Fire of Bergen – which razed the city centre to the ground from Murallmenningen to Christies Gate, coming to a halt just before the central fire station. By then it had destroyed so much that Bergen took on a whole new look in the 1920s.

But in former times the locals had a tendency to ignore public orders and rebuild their wooden houses just as they had been before the fire. As such, some of the areas and streets of medieval Bergen have been preserved, not least in Vågs-bunnen. Elsewhere you will find wide streets designed to slow down fire – without ever having much effect!

Despite its history of fires, Bergen is still one of Europe's largest wooden cities, if not the largest. Wooden houses wend their way up over Fjellsiden behind the Fløibanen station, and clump together at Nøstet, in Skuteviken and Rosegrenden in Sandviken – to name but a few areas where visitors can see houses as they were in days of yore. And even the smallest of houses were often inspired by the residences and pavilions of the wealthy, many of which have survived to the present day.

All in all, Bergen is an exciting city for those with an interest in architecture. Passing the "Bergen empire", with its wealth of detail, red-tiled roofs on white houses, and historic stone and brick buildings, the walk from Kalfaret to Nordnes and Sandviken is well worth taking.

Fotografisk atelier

Brand Signal

Söre Steinkjellersmauet

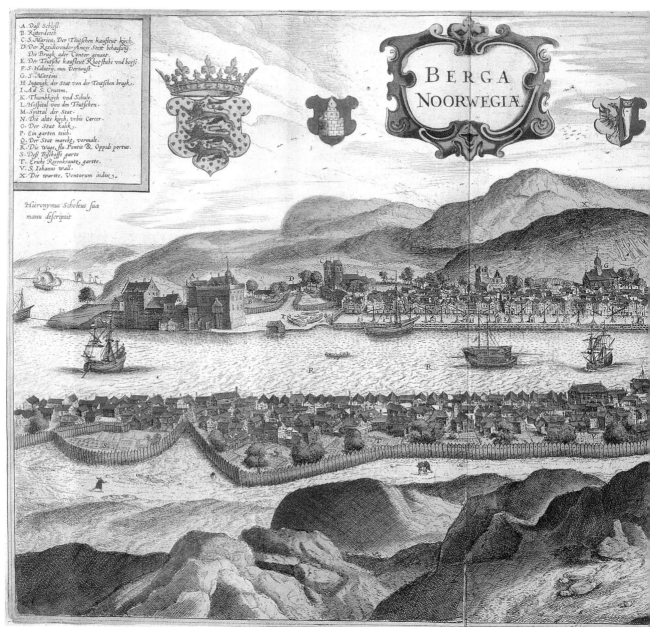

The Scholeus Print. The oldest and best-known view of Bergen was drawn by Hieronimus Scholeus and etched in copper by Franz Hogenberg. It occupied a double page in a book published in 1588, one of a series of six volumes issued between 1572 and 1618. The Scholeus Print was to remain the international image of Bergen for almost 200 years.

GUILDS AND LEARNING

Although Bergen may not literally have risen Aphrodite-like out of the waves, one of the city's many poets and songwriters described her as the "princess of the sea" — and it is not difficult to see why. The city was, in its own way, born of the sea and has lived off the sea for over 900 years.

It all started with the harbour. There were already settlers living along the water's edge when king Olav Kyrre decided to set up a "trading post" in 1070, thus founding what was to become Bergen.

Twelfth century Bergen developed into an important European trading centre, establishing a connection between western and northern Norway and the rest of the world.

Norway's first residential city and capital, Bergen went on over the centuries to become the largest city in Norway, and indeed the Northern countries.

Although home to the kings of Norway, Bergen did not have a large and rich hinterland and thus trade and craft became sources of income. As such, the city catered not only for tradesmen, ship-owners and sea-

Hanseatic cog, 1500.

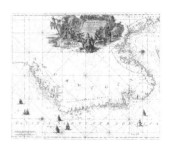

Dutch map, probably 18th-century.

farers, but also for craftsmen. Specialists in their various fields, the craftsmen had their own areas and quarters in the city and formed their own guilds. The oldest of the Norwegian guilds is the Bergen Gullsmedlaug (Bergen Goldsmiths' Guild) which dates back to 1568.

Today Bergen is just as much a centre for learning and knowledge as a centre of commerce. Established a little after the last world war, the University of Bergen builds on traditions from the Bergen Museum, founded in 1825. The city is also home to Norway's first business school, the Directorate of Fisheries and its Institute of Marine Research. It also has a college of art, craft and design, colleges of engineering and education, a music academy, the internationally recognised Christian Michelsen Institute and a centre for advanced technology with a diverse range of activities.

Bergen has been through good times and bad times over the centuries. But even though the king moved the capital to Oslo and the city had periods of both prosperity and depression, Bergen managed to retain its position as a cultural, maritime and trading centre — a city that is just a little bit different, populated by people who like to be a little different from other Norwegians.

THE GATEWAY TO THE FJORDS OF NORWAY

"When in Rome, do as the Romans do." And when in Bergen, make sure you visit the fjords! There is a reason why Bergen has been termed "Fjord Capital" and "Gateway to the fjords". The city is ideally positioned between the majesty of the Sogne fjord and the charm of the Hardanger fjord. During the summer months there is a veritable range of cruise boats heading both north and south. Closer to Bergen there are countless smaller fjords and skerries — a paradise for boat enthusiasts. The Sogne fjord is the world's longest and deepest fjord. Most of the people living here, live on the north bank. The inner part of the fjord is divided into several smaller fjord arms; the Fjærland fjord, the Sogndal fjord and the Luster fjord to the north, the Årdal fjord to the east and the Lærdal fjord, the Aurland- and the Nærøy fjord to the south. There are numerous waterfalls along the mountainsides of the Nærøy fjord. At one point (just south of Bakka) the fjord is less than 500 metres wide.

Fjordlandscape with rowing boat in Osa, Hardanger.

The Hardanger fjord is the longest fjord in Hordaland county. The main part of the fjord is 6 - 11 kilometres wide, but the fjord arms are more narrow. The deepest point, 830 metres, is measured in the Ytre Samla fjord, and the depth of the mouth of the fjord is approximately 500 metres. The Hardanger fjord stretches from Seløy and Ånuglo and northeast towards Odda. With its glaciers, waterfalls and mountain peeks, the Hardanger fjord has been a source of inspiration for several artists. But anyone can become lyrical at the sight of the fruit trees in blossom down by the very edge of the water while the glistening white snow adorns the distant mountain peaks …

The Nærøy Fjord.

The Nærøy Fjord.

Vøringsfossen waterfall.

Låtefoss waterfall.

Flåmsdalen and the Flåm Railway, a branch of the Bergen Line.

© N.W. Damm & Søn AS
N-0055 Oslo

Tel: +47 24 05 10 00

This book is published in cooperation with
Bergen Tourist Board

2. publication, 5. edition

Author: Lotte Schønfelder
Design: Bergsnov, Mellbye & Rosenbaum as
Coverdesign: Sissel Holt Boniface
Printed in Denmark 2007
Translation: Berlitz A/S
Translation German edition: Marlis Ehl

Captions for full-page illustrations:
Page 1. Statsraad Lehmkuhl, Bergen's magnificent sailing vessel, moored at Bryggen.
Pages 2-3. Bergen city centre.
Pages 4-5. Old Bergen.
Pages 6-7. Bryggen with Fløyen in the background.
Pages 24-25. Bergen seen from Fløyen on a winter day.
Pages 60-61. The Aurlandsfjord.
Pages 62-63. Otternes village square, Aurland.
Page 64. The blossoming orchards of Hardanger.

PHOTOGRAPHERS:
Top = A. Top left = B. Top right = C.
Bottom = D. Bottom left = E. Bottom right = F.
Middle = G. Middle left = H. Middle right = I

Samfoto:
Bård Løken: Front page B, 58A, 59AD, 60-61, 62-63, 59A.
Jørn Areklett Omre: 34E, 52.
Pål Hermansen: 20-21A, 58D.
Helge Sunde: Front page F, 11BF, 13, 24-25, 26F, 32, 33, 40C, 49AI, 53C.
J.B. Olsen/R.Sørensen: 12CF, 57F.
Stig Tronvold: 56-57A, 64.
Espen Bratlie: 12B.
Jan Arve Dale: 45A

Per Eide: Front page E, 8CEF, 12G, 14-15, 17D, 19, 22D, 23A, 26, 27F, 28D, 29E, 30A, 34B, 38AE, 40B, 42, 43E, 51, 53G.

Willy Haraldsen: Front page H, 6-7, 8BC, 16-17A, 20EF, 22A, 26E, 29F, 30F, 36, 37ADF, 44A, 45E, 50E, 53B.

Billedbyrået A/S:
Øystein Klakegg: 2-3, 8D, 30E, 38D, 44F, 50B.
Pål Hoff: 8A, 18, 23F, 27A, 28BE, 29D, 31, 38FH 49F.
Ottar Uthaug: 8, 35.
Robin Strand: Front page H, 10, 26H, 38F, 40E, 41A.
Per Nybø: 1, 21F, 38E, 41EF, back page.
Harald Bjørnstad: Front page C, 38E, 39, 40F.
R. Hjertholm: 43F, 49I.

Knutsens Fotosenter: 43A.

Jon Fjeldstad: 23F.

O. Væring: 48.

Bergen Sjøfartsmuseum: 55FI.

Museet Lysøen: 44E.

Bergen Museum: 55B, 54, 55A.

Bergen Kunstmuseum: 49H.

Statens Kunstmuser, Stockholm: 47A.